ANIMAL SCAVENGERS

Tasmanian Devils

SANDRA MARKLE

LERNER PUBLICATIONS COMPANY / MINNEAPOLIS

The Animal World Is Full of SCAVENGERS.

Scavengers are the cleanup crew who find and eat carrion (dead animals) in order to survive. Every day, animals are born and animals die. Without scavengers, the bodies of dead animals would rot away slowly. The decaying flesh would smell bad and take up space. It could also pollute water and attract flies and other disease-carrying insects. Fortunately, scavengers everywhere eat dead and dying animals before they have time to rot. On the small cluster of islands called Tasmania, a part of Australia, this group of scavengers includes Tasmanian devils. *In fact, Tasmania is the only place in the world these unique animals live!*

It's a March afternoon, and it is autumn in Tasmania. Days are short at this time of year. The light filtering through the eucalyptus forest is fading fast. As if the gathering darkness is a cue, the young female Tasmanian devil pokes her head out of her burrow. She sniffs the air and looks around before venturing all the way out. She's about the size of an English bulldog and just as solidly built, with a strong body and sturdy short legs. She also has a fat, tapered tail that's about half as long as the rest of her body.

She takes another quick look around. With her big ears perked to catch sounds, the female Tasmanian devil sets off in search of a meal. Tasmanian devils' hindquarters slope. And their hind legs are shorter than their front legs. So the animals have a rolling gait. It's a pace this female can keep up for long distances.

After a while, she stops to scent mark her trail before trotting on. This is her home range, the area the young female lives in and knows well. She doesn't try to keep other Tasmanian devils out. But she does mark her trails. Sometimes she does this by depositing her scent along with her wastes. This time, though, she squats and drags her rear end across the ground. She has special anal glands that produce an oily yellow fluid with her unique scent.

When she's finished, she stands still, listening. Like all Tasmanian devils, she has very good hearing. She can detect sounds as far as one-half mile (nearly one kilometer) away. Her ears turn, helping her focus on the eerie screams of other devils. It could be devils competing for food. Eager to claim a share, the young female devil trots off, following her ears toward the source of the sound.

When she gets close, the young female also picks up the scent of other devils. A big male has been here, eaten his fill of the carrion, and gone. An older, bigger female devil has now claimed the scraps. At first, as the young female approaches, the older female continues her meal. She crunches a leg bone in her powerful jaws.

But when the young female devil grabs a scrap for herself, she becomes a rival. The two females face off and scream at each other. The shrill, eerie sounds rise and fall like sirens. Then the young female grabs another mouthful. The bigger, older female attacks, nipping her rival's rump. The two females face off again, growling and screaming. The young female devil could stay. She could continue to squabble over mouthfuls, but she chooses to retreat.

The young female only goes as far away as a fallen log. Climbing on top of it, she screams again and stamps her feet. The older female doesn't seem concerned as she returns to her meal. She keeps on eating until the young female slips up to try for another mouthful. Then the older female charges and drives the youngster away again. This time, the young female gives up and continues her search for food.

It's night before her nose again picks up the scent of rotting flesh. This time, it's a dead kangaroo. The young female gnaws through the kangaroo's belly, where the tough skin is thinnest. Then she pokes her head inside and pulls out a chunk of juicy liver. She gulps this morsel down without chewing. Then she noses in for more. She eats quickly in case any other scavengers, especially any big male devils, arrive to claim a share. Male devils may be nearly twice as big as females.

The young female devil eats her fill. Before she is finished, she will have eaten almost half of her weight in meat. It's also starting to get light, so the young female waddles into a hollow log. She sleeps there until the sun is high overhead. Then she waddles into the open, stretches out on a patch of sun-warmed dirt, and goes back to sleep. It's late afternoon before the young female wakes up again.

She lopes to a nearby water hole, wades in, and drinks her fill. She stays in the water, cooling off. Suddenly, another female devil arrives. Always competitive, the two face off. The new arrival screams a threat. The young female devil screams her response. For a few minutes, neither female budges. Finally, still screaming, the new arrival eases forward until she can reach the water. Between screams, both females drink. Eventually, both female devils go their separate ways.

The young devil travels through the forest, listening and sniffing. Once again, sounds guide her to a meal, a dead wombat. Wombats are a burrowing relative of the koala. She finds that three female devils are already competing for shares of this meal.

They scream as she claims a place to eat. The competitor closest to her nips at her shoulder as she noses in. The young female screams but doesn't retreat. There's plenty of food here, so the competitor moves over.

Each Tasmanian devil has a ring of long, touch-sensitive whiskers around its face. So the scavengers space themselves just out of touch. Still, the female devils continue to nip at each other throughout their meal. Each ends up with a few bite wounds as well as a full belly.

That night, the young female Tasmanian devil goes to an abandoned wombat burrow that she's used before. She pulls out the old dried grass and ferns that line the den and drags in fresh green bedding. The next night, she doesn't leave the den to forage (look for food). Just a few weeks before, she mated with one of the big males sharing her home range. The young Tasmanian devil, snug in her den, gives birth.

At birth the newborn devils are as tiny as grains of rice. They are naked, and their eyes are closed. They must wiggle into a pouch on their mother's belly to continue developing. Animals that give birth to young that finish their development inside a pouch are called marsupials. The marsupial mother doesn't help her babies into the pouch. Only the strongest babies complete the journey. Female Tasmanian devils have only four teats to provide the milk the babies need. The first four babies to latch onto a teat are the only ones that survive. They grow bigger quickly and soon begin to grow their fur coats.

With her babies inside her pouch, the young female continues her routine of foraging for food each night. Sometimes she's even able to catch fresh food like this pigeon, which had been wounded by a sparrow hawk.

While she's foraging, the female keeps her pouch tightly closed by squeezing muscles to press the edges together. Even when winter comes, her growing babies stay safe and warm. Sometimes when she stops, she checks on her babies and licks inside her pouch to wash them and clean out their wastes.

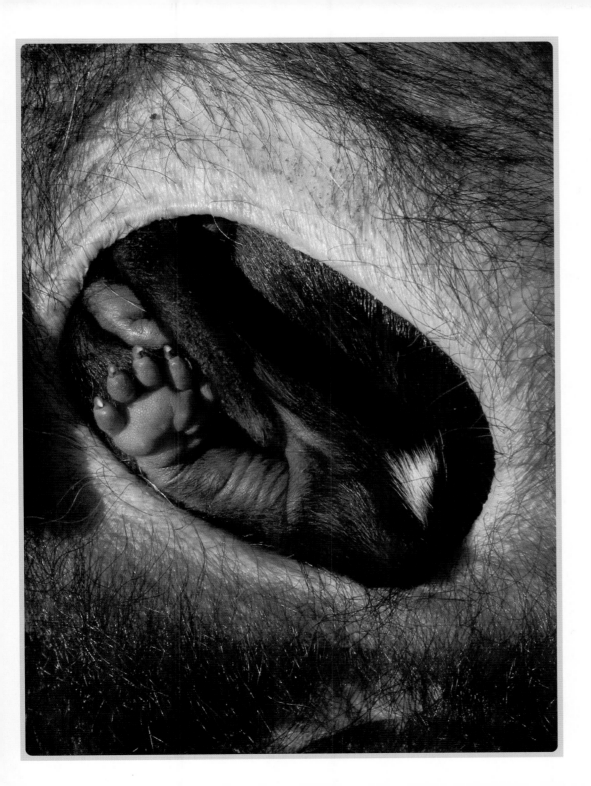

The young female devil returns each day to the wombat burrow she's claimed for her den. This is where she'll raise her youngsters when they're ready to leave her pouch. Within a month, they're about the size of walnuts. After two months, they're as big as adult mice. By the time they are three months old, they're about the size of newborn kittens. Then it's a tight fit for them inside the pouch.

When the baby devils are about fifteen weeks old, the male and three little females come out from their mother's pouch for the first time. They're now too big to stay squeezed together inside the small space. The pouch is also too warm for the fur-covered youngsters. They will poke their heads into the pouch to nurse, though. They'll continue to feed that way until they leave their mother and go off on their own.

The babies are now too big to share the pouch. So they take turns nursing. True to their devil nature, though, they don't share well. Anytime their mother returns to the den, the baby devils get into a wrestling match. The male will one day grow to be much bigger than his sisters. But for now, the siblings are all about the same size. None can win on size alone, so it's usually the most aggressive youngster that gets to nurse first.

One day while the female devil is away foraging, another female finds her burrow. Other female devils are predators of young devils. They'll kill and eat any youngsters they can find. Hearing strange noises, the youngsters crawl into the network of tunnels they've dug beyond their nursery chamber. Luckily, the young mother returns home just in time. Screaming with rage, she charges in to defend her family. The intruder runs away rather than risk being wounded. Then the mother makes soft noises to assure her youngsters that it's safe to come out and nurse.

The snow has melted, and it's springtime in the forest. The young devils are almost five months old, and they are starting to cut their teeth. They chew on anything they can grab, including their siblings, their mother, and scraps of skin and meat she carries home to them.

The youngsters are bolder too. When their mother leaves to forage for food, they often crawl to the den entrance to wait for her. There they peer into the night. They sniff the interesting scents of the world outside their nursery. Sometimes, when hunger makes them impatient, the young devils scream for their mother.

One night, after their mother leaves, the bravest female of the brood leaves her squabbling siblings behind in the den. Outside, the little female's urge to explore lures her beyond the den entrance. A masked owl perched in a tree overhead spots the young devil.

Some inner sense makes the little female look up. When she spots the hunter spreading its wings, she scurries for the den entrance. She scoots inside just in time to escape the owl's swooping attack.

By the time the young devils are about six months old, they're eating solid food. They find a lot of insects to eat and occasionally catch a mouse. But their mother still supplies most of their food. The young female devil continues to nurse her offspring. She also brings home meat for them. In true devil fashion, the siblings squabble and compete for the biggest share of each meal.

One night when their mother is away, the siblings, as usual, start to fight. Their noisy squabbling attracts a spotted-tailed quoll. Stealthily, this housecat-sized hunter slips up on the young devils. When one little female drags off a chunk of meat to eat alone, the quoll overpowers and kills her.

The female Tasmanian devil continues to feed her remaining three babies until they are about nine months old. Then one night, she leaves for good. She heads off into parts of her home range she hasn't traveled since their birth. The male stays at the burrow for two days. He becomes restless and bullies his sisters more than usual as his hunger grows. Finally, he leaves. He follows his senses to the smell of carrion, which he knows means food. He has no problem feeding himself.

The two sisters remain at the burrow for another day. Hunger finally drives them out in search of food. One is caught and killed by an owl. The remaining female escapes. For two nights, she forages without success. Finally, she follows her nose to a dead wallaby. She instinctively knows to dig into the body where the skin is thinnest. The little female devil quickly gulps down all she can eat and crunches up the bones. She has become the newest devil to join Tasmania's cleanup crew.

Looking Back

- Look at the Tasmanian devil's teeth on page 8. Then look for other pictures where the teeth are visible. Do you see why devils can't grind up their food? Their teeth are all cone-shaped. This shape is good only to snip off meat and crunch up bones. Then the animals swallow chunks, and their digestive system finishes the job of breaking it down.

- Take another look at the Tasmanian devils on page 16, and check out their tails. Devils store fat in their tails and use up this reserve when food is scarce. Researchers check their health by measuring whether their tails are fat or skinny.

- Look again at the young devil on page 31. She probably could have stayed safe just by staying still. Then her mainly black coat would make her look like a shadow. Her white markings would also break up her body shape, making it even harder for a predator to spot. Read *Animal Predators: Killer Whales* also by Sandra Markle to see how being black and white helps one kind of predator sneak up on its prey.

Glossary

ANAL GLANDS: body parts in an animal's hind end that produce chemicals that an animal deposits or sprays out to communicate

BURROW: a tunnel and any connected chambers that an animal digs

CARRION: a dead animal that a scavenger eats

FORAGE: to hunt for food

HOME RANGE: an area where an animal lives and forages for food

PREDATOR: an animal that hunts and eats other animals in order to survive

PREY: an animal that a predator catches to eat

SCAVENGER: an animal that feeds on dead animals

SCENT: an odor left behind by an animal

Further Information

BOOKS

Arnold, Caroline. *Australian Animals.* New York: Harper Collins, 2000. Organized by different habitats, this book provides a view of the natural setting Tasmanian devils call home in Tasmania, plus some of the other animals that are their neighbors. This also includes a look at other parts of Australia, helping readers understand Tasmania's location in the world.

Darling, Kathy. *Tasmanian Devils: On Location.* New York: Harper Collins, 1992. The author provides personal observations of Tasmanian devil behavior plus additional information on life history.

Steele, Christy. *Tasmanian Devils: Animals of the Rain Forest.* Chicago: Raintree, 2003. This title offers an introduction to this animal, its features, and behavior.

VIDEOS

Living Eden: Tasmania: Land of Devils (PBS Home Video, 2001). This video gives a visually beautiful overview of Tasmania.

National Geographic's Australia (National Geographic, 2003). This is a visual introduction to Australia and its wildlife.

WEBSITE

Tasmania Parks & Wildlife Service.
http://www.parks.tas.gov.au/wildlife/mammals/devil.html. Hear the eerie cries of the Tasmanian devil at this website.

Index

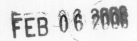

With love always for my husband, Skip Jeffery

The author would like to thank Dr. Menna Jones and Dr. Heather Hesterman, research fellows at the University of Tasmania and wildlife biologists working for the Nature Conservation Branch of the Department of Primary Industries, Water and Environment, Tasmania, for sharing their expertise and enthusiasm. The author would also like to express a special thank you to Skip Jeffery for his help and support during the creative process.

Photo Acknowledgments
The photographs in this book are used with permission of: © Dave Watts/naturepl.com, pp. 1, 16, 29, 31, 32, 37; © D. Parer & E. Parer-Cook/AUSCAPE, pp. 3, 11, 19, 21, 35; © Mitsuaki Iwago/Minden Pictures, p. 5; Photodisc Royalty Free by Getty Images, pp. 7, 10; © Reg Morrison/AUSCAPE, p. 8; © Mark Spencer/AUSCAPE, p. 9; © Kathie Atkinson/Oxford Scientific Films, p. 13; © Dennis Harding/AUSCAPE, p. 15; © NHPA/Dave Watts, pp. 18, 26, 33; © John Cancalosi/AUSCAPE, p. 20; © Dave Watts/ANTPhoto.com, pp. 23, 25; © Eric and David Hosking/CORBIS, p. 30. Front cover: Photodisc Royalty Free by Getty Images. Back cover (top): © D. Parer & E. Parer-Cook/Auscape/Minden Pictures. Back cover (bottom): *Army Ants*: © Christian Ziegler; *Hyenas*: © Richard du Toit/naturepl.com; *Jackals*: © Beverly Joubert/National Geographic/Getty Images; *Tasmanian Devils*: Photodisc Royalty Free by Getty Images; *Vultures*: © Chris Hellier/CORBIS; *Wolverines*: © Daniel J. Cox/naturalexposures.com.

Lerner Publications Company, Inc.
A division of Lerner Publishing Group
241 First Avenue North
Minneapolis, MN 55401 U.S.A.

Website address: www.lernerbooks.com

Library of Congress Cataloging-in-Publication Data

Markle, Sandra.
   Tasmanian devils / by Sandra Markle.
     p.   cm. — (Animal scavengers)
   Includes bibliographical references and index.
   ISBN-13: 978−0−8225−3199−9 (lib. bdg. : alk. paper)
   ISBN-10: 0−8225−3199−2 (lib. bdg. : alk. paper)
   1. Tasmanian devil—Juvenile literature. I. Title. II. Series: Markle, Sandra. Animal scavengers.
   QL737.M33M27 2005
   599.2'7—dc22
                                    2004029671

Manufactured in the United States of America
1 2 3 4 5 6 − DP − 10 09 08 07 06 05

READ ANIMAL PREDATORS, A *BOOKLIST* TOP 10 YOUTH NONFICTION SERIES BY SANDRA MARKLE

Crocodiles
Great White Sharks
Killer Whales
Lions
Owls
Polar Bears
Wolves